The Genre Writer's Book of Writing Prompts & Story Ideas

540 Creative Writing Prompts in the Genres of Fantasy, Sci-Fi, Mystery & Thriller, Horror & Supernatural, and Memoir

Created and compiled by the Mayday Writing Collective

INTRODUCTION

As every writer knows, there are days when the words come easily and days when they do not—and sometimes days when no words come at all. It can be maddening to go from effortlessly creating your own vivid worlds or telling your personal story with such intensity that it feels like you're reliving it again to feeling empty and creatively impotent.

But never fear. The Mayday writing team is here to help. We are a tight-knit team of genre writers representing three continents and five countries, and between us we have written more than a hundred books. We know the pain of writer's block firsthand and we have discovered a powerful solution: Writing prompts and story ideas.

Sure, you can buy books of 2,000 or 5,000 or even 10,000 writing prompts for pennies nowadays, but you get what you pay for—generic, lifeless prompts that feel like they were written by a computer (perhaps they were! Now *there's* a story idea). What the Mayday writing team has put together are 540 prompts—108 prompts in five genres—that represent months of brainstorming and hours of creative discussion among our writers.

Why 108? Is it because of the number's significance in Hinduism and Buddhism? Or its appearance in martial arts? A secret connection to the number of cards in a deck of UNO?

Truth be told, we were just drawn to it. We hope you find it as enchanting a number as we do.

We'd love to see what stories you spin from the prompts in this book. Share them with the world by using the hashtag **#writingmayday** on your social network of choice.

Happy writing!

USING THIS BOOK

You're welcome to use this book any way you see fit, but the Mayday writing team has a few suggestions to help you get the most of out of all 540 writing prompts:

The Random Roll. This is our favorite way to pick a prompt. Go to a random number site such as random.org (or roll some dice!) and generate two random numbers, one between 1 and 5 and another between 1 and 108. The first number is the genre to write in—Fantasy (1), Sci-Fi (2), Mystery & Thriller (3), Horror & Supernatural (4), Memoir (5)—and the second is the prompt in that genre. If you want to restrict yourself to a specific genre, just leave off the first roll. As you work through prompts, mark off their stamps to keep track of which ones you've completed.

Once you have your prompt, you need to set how long you'll be writing for. This is where our signature **90-7-30 system** comes in. Here's how it works:

If you're a beginning writer or you're short on time, start with **90 seconds** of nonstop writing per prompt. This easy-to-achieve time limit lets you stretch your writing muscles on a regular basis, and the nonstop requirement keeps your mind from wandering.

If you're ready for something more, it's time to move on to **7 minutes** per prompt. You should still aim to write as continuously as possible during these 7 minutes, but you should also seek to produce a cohesive passage, with a clear beginning and middle (and end, if you can fit it in there).

When you're feeling limbered up, go ahead and try for a whopping **30 minutes** of writing. It's likely you'll have a few pauses here and there, and that's okay—the focus of the 30 minute writing block is dedication and discipline. Stay put for the entire duration (if life allows) and make sure you avoid checking email, Facebook, Instagram, Tik Tok, or any of the other million distractions that are trying to keep you from writing.

You can even revisit each prompt with different 90-7-30 time limits, exploring past ideas or giving life to new ones. Be creative, be daring, be you!

Keep your writing organized. It helps to have one place where you do all of your writing so that you can refer to it any time you want. Maybe that's a notebook, a computer document, or even the notes app on your phone. Our personal favorite are Rollbahn's spiral-bound notebooks for physical writing and the ultra-convenient Google Docs for digital work.

Set a goal. You don't have to write everyday (though we recommend it!) but you should commit to writing a set number of times a week and sticking to it. It will be hard at first, but writing is like every other skill—you need regular practice for it to improve. And if you decide on 90 seconds of writing per prompt, that's less than 5 minutes a week. You can spare that, right?

The more you write, the better you'll get. Take it from us and the collective tens of thousands of pages we've written. You can do this.

BEFORE YOU GET STARTED...

Through out this book, you'll see these shapes quite often:

These are part of the Mayday team's **90-7-30 system** mentioned in the USING THIS BOOK section. They appear after every single prompt as both a reminder on how to use the prompts and a checklist. Consider filling in, crossing off, or even putting a date next to each stamp as you progress through this book. Not only will this help you track your progress, but it will point you towards new challenges and will keep you pushing yourself to new writing heights.

FANTASY WRITING PROMPTS

"Fantasy is a necessary ingredient in living, it's a way of looking at life through the wrong end of the telescope."

- Dr. Seuss

1. A talking cape is convincing its owners they can fly, drawing the attention of the Artifacts Investigation Unit.

2. An ancient mask offers whoever wears it tremendous strength, but records everything they do while wearing it. You put on the mask and realize the last wearer used it to commit a murder.

3. A machinist specializing in magic-infused devices is hired to build a transporter.

4. I'd never met one of the snakewomen before, but I knew their skill with magic was unparalleled. That meant if the negotiation went south, I was a dead man.

5. Create a superpower with drawbacks that are almost worse than the benefits.

6. In a quiet tavern on the outskirts of a sleepy village, a traveling wizard arrives, looking battleworn. He hands you the bladeless hilt of a knife and says, "Well, what are you waiting for?"

7. They say there is a cursed minute of a cursed hour of a cursed day each year when the tower turns to gold and all who look upon it will die by the next full moon. And we idiots were staring right at the damned thing.

8. Mystical historian and mage lobbyist Redolo comes to town, seeking exciting stories about near encounters with death. You find him one evening and explain you've got the story of a lifetime...

9. Going through your deceased grandfather's belongings, you find a strange token whose origins you can't identify. You carry it with you and accidentally use it to enter the subway one day, revealing an underground world hidden from plain sight.

10. Fortune tellers are being murdered all over the city. A former customer who has seen several of them reveals that their predictions have always come true.

11. Two rings allow their wearers to feel one another's physical pain, with an unexpected effect when one person wears both rings.

12. When the king's grimoire is replaced with a fake, he begins to suspect those closest to him of having made the switch.

13. A retired superhero is suffering PTSD after having saved the lives of millions a decade earlier.

14. Books are disappearing from libraries across the country. The suspected culprit? A 10-year-old boy whose birth date is 200 years in the past.

15. Self-taught wizard and private investigator Nate Spellward is hired to find the source of a magical drug that's leaving witches and warlocks dead all over town.

16. Calling us Hunters is a convenient but incorrect way to describe us. We don't hunt, and we don't kill. We simply put broken things back together again.

17. Describe a monster that lives in an underground maze and survives off lost travelers.

18. You've worked your way up through the ranks of the city guard when you are finally appointed a position guarding a lesser-known royal family member. By the end of your first day, the royal will be dead and you will be framed for their murder.

19. I understood the fallen gods better once I saw them for what they were: laid off from their jobs.

20. A mad king makes a deal with a dangerous race of giants in exchange for a terrifying weapon.

21. You are a monster hunter contracted to kill a sea serpent that has been spotted off the coast. As you begin your preparations, the serpent emerges from the water and offers to make you a deal...

22. They say you never see the Slea before they kill you, but you do smell them. Iron, sulphur, and rotten fruit. When those scents filled my nose, I knew I was in for the fight of my life.

23. You're on vacation in a big city, out at a bar late at night. The patron next to you leaves and the rest of the bar reveals that they are angels and demons in disguise. Somehow you have gone unnoticed as the only human left.

24. A team of superheroes are disillusioned with their country's ideals and decide to defect and become terrorists instead.

25. The entire city of London starts slipping backwards in time, causing living creatures to grow younger and even buildings to revert to their former conditions.

26. While you're working late one night at a store for mystic curiosities, a customer with deep pockets arrives looking for an off-the-menu item.

27. In a land where knowing someone's secret name allows you to control them, a woman stumbles upon an arcane directory, offering her almost total control of everyone she encounters.

28. A master ranger is caught in an unexpectedly sophisticated woodland trap while on patrol, and must figure out a way to free herself before her would-be captors return.

29. The Emotionalist traced her finger along the door's jamb, threading it through with fear.

30. Logic Spinners, craftsman who imbue everyday objects with magic, find their work suddenly in high demand when a rival kingdom begins building magical weapons of war.

31. A mild-mannered corporate drone finds a six shooter in his mailbox one day that, to his shock, can speak. It tells him it has six people for him to kill.

32. I hated visiting the arachnomancer's home.

33. In modern day Cleveland, a race of Medusa-like Gorgons is discovered living among the populace, using their petrification ability to break into the construction market.

34. In the chaos of the War of the Third Eye, Captain Bashiri must face down the possessed and resurrected corpse of his long dead sister, once known as Jhara the Unseen.

35. It was never supposed rain in the living city. Our time was up.

36. My dealings with the Qi-tarl had always been transactional in nature and nothing more. That's why it made no sense that their elder asked for me as her champion.

37. Describe the entryway to a forbidden temple rumored to contain a legendary monster.

38. Out at the Karthasin sea, a swarm of flying manta rays attacks a cargo ship, attracted by a mysterious package onboard.

39. The eye swiveled around in the sword's hilt, seeking its next target.

40. A swarm of sentient flies descends upon a local church, causing a retired bishop to face a horror he hasn't encountered in decades.

41. A merchant's Master of Coin finds a discrepancy in the merchant's books and uncovers a dark scandal.

42. Describe a hidden city that exists deep in an impenetrable jungle that's filled with arcane magic.

43. During a mass exodus from a collapsing Dwarven kingdom in the mountains, a hideous creature awakens and begins stalking travelers in the nearby countryside.

44. In the politics-laden kingdom of Domm-trell, a rising mage finds himself put on trial for treason.

45. You're at a bank when an attempted robbing begins. It's then you discover you have a curious superpower: for as long as you hold your breath, time stops. How do you foil the robbers?

46. An ancient suit of armor housed at the Met is broken open in an accident and reveals a cryptic map.

47. When an assassination attempt goes wrong and a lookalike to the queen is murdered, bounty hunters across the city find themselves in the crosshairs of the royal guard. But working together they soon discover the lookalike was the target all along.

48. The crowd cheered as Ultrick and I stared each other down, our blades drawn. This was the fight they'd been waiting for all day, but they had no idea what we had in store for them.

49. No one hunts wights, not really. You just kill as many as you can before they kill you.

50. Every thousand years, the fabled Cloudbeast descends from the sky and selects a new ruler. This time, it's a year early, bearing a grim omen.

51. Describe an opulent palace belonging to a retired wizard.

52. Yes, I was one of Gorloth's minions. The rumors are true. But despite his bloodlust, Gorloth had his redeeming qualities too.

53. A hermit who has remained in his apartment for the last several weeks wakes up one morning to discover a thick length of rope running through his home, all the way to the drain of his bathtub. He gives the rope a tug and when he does he feels a tug back in return.

54. A subway train pulls into Times Square that is from September 10th, 2001—passengers and all.

55. Tathos was the most gifted cleric in all the three realms, but for him to work his miracles he had to be drunk.

56. Rumors of a goblin invasion are spreading through the city, provoking the city's army to begin mobilizing a preemptive strike against a nearby goblin settlement. Only you know that you and your tavern buddies started the rumors.

57. Numbers start appearing on people's foreheads, some counting up, others down. Yours is the only one set to zero.

58. From his belt hung a pouch filled with heavy, iron coins, and on each coin was a name—one for each of us in his crew. It's how he kept track of us. How he controlled us.

59. A pair of sorceresses form a bloodoath of loyalty that's put to the test when a dashing stranger rides into town.

60. Vicrenza said she'd found the horn in the ruinlands, but it was in far too good condition for that.

61. Describe a mystical weapon that a warrior on horseback would use.

62. I nocked the arrow and held my breath. I'd only have one chance to blind the beast.

63. Upon dying, corporate drone John Lazby is given a choice: life in limbo, or a return to Earth with a mission to save a murderer's life.

64. As the trade war between rival merchant houses heats up, one thief finds himself in possession of a forbidden artifact.

65. I woke up in another body after a long, dark night.

66. My mentor always said never to look a cyclops in the eye. Now I knew why.

67. Due to a mix up at the store, you accidentally go home with a magical spice rack. What are some of the spices you find there?

68. When the princess's childhood cat, Cream, is hit by a stray transformation spell and becomes twenty times its size, only the princess can keep Cream from wreaking havoc throughout the castle.

69. A radio station is discovered that can tune into the afterlife—but only in proximity to the speaker's corpse. A landrush ensues for cemetery plots.

70. An expert practitioner of nostalagiacraft is kidnapped, their blood used by a magical syndicate to interrogate their enemies.

71. We crested the hill and in the distance saw the gaping maw that led into the undersea. Then I felt the first drops of rain and knew we had to push forward, despite our fears.

72. While on a vacation in Eastern Europe, a couple wanders off a hiking trail and discovers a cave that leads to an abandoned underground city.

73. After a long journey, you enter a smoke-filled pub to rest your feet and have a drink. In the corner is a blind man who somehow seems to know your name and who offers to sell you a map.

74. An agoraphobic archivist must smuggle documents between two distant cities, traversing a great wilderness that has been left behind technologically and societally.

75. Hexmancer Phi is going through a rut, with all her hexes backfiring in disappointing ways. Seeing her bad luck, she comes up with a crazy plan: to hex herself. But it goes terribly wrong.

76. A man cloaked in rags appears out of nowhere in front of the King's throne, whispering a message before he dies: "The Twisted will remain hidden no longer."

77. A hunting expedition goes awry when its organizer reveals they are hunting a mythological beast.

78. When the sailor Flakros is lost at sea and saved by mermaids, he discovers they have a fate worse than death in store for him.

79. The leathery old men and shoeless children all told the same legend about the tunnel in the mountain.

80. Pierre turned the coin over in his fingers three times, each turn revealing a new face upon its silvery surface.

81. You are recruited to join a group of supernaturally gifted thieves to break into a bank and steal a safe deposit box. You claim to have no powers, but the group's organizer informs you that won't be true for much longer.

82. In a rural country home, a closet keeps growing rooms inside it each time its door is closed and opened again.

83. When a massacre occurs at an annual carnival, the royal family sends a witch to investigate the cause. What she discovers will leave the entire kingdom feeling unsafe.

84. While townspeople are shopping at an outdoor local market, a woman with bird wings falls from the sky.

85. At the Magical Protection Agency, a warlock proposes a plan to claim Australia as a magic-only island.

86. You are a therapist with a very strange clientele: you only treat mystical creatures trying to acclimate to a human world.

87. A woman wakes up on her 40th birthday to find she is 14 again and is about to relive the day of her best friend's death.

88. Three warring kingdoms, three dead princes—his work was almost done.

89. Describe ancient seaside ruins without using the sense of sight.

90. A mysterious carnival comes to town, and a wizened gentleman offers you the chance to spin a roulette wheel that will grant you a random magical ability. You spin and are disappointed to receive...

91. It was a sweltering summer day in South Jersey when the devil came to town to ask us for a favor.

92. A group of D-list supervillains form a collective to cause petty crimes at a scale impossible for their rival superheroes to counteract.

93. I paced back and forth in the basement of the inn and stopped when I heard the scratching steps of the Nightwalker above me.

94. Each of the seven deadly sins reveals itself to be a paranormal being among humanity, and for each of them a human champion has been chosen to stand against them. You have been chosen to fight Pride.

95. The famed dragonhunter Gregario has a problem—all his stories are lies, and he's about to be found out.

96. A cryptic message is left painted in blood across the inside of a castle's gates, warning all inside that they have two nights to leave or face death.

97. After a Category 5 hurricane touches down on Florida, an entire suburban town's population goes missing without any damage to the town itself.

98. An underground expedition goes awry, creating a sinkhole that slowly starts expanding. After years of this, one day it suddenly stops, and a voice emanates from the sinkhole, calling for your name.

99. The woods nestled between two mountains are rumored to be haunted. A band of ragtag adventurers is hired to find out the truth and discover a crafty old woman is behind the rumors.

100. You move into a new home and discover a small hidden door at the back of one of the closets. When you go through this door, you appear as a ghost for twenty minutes somewhere in the world.

101. For the first time in human history, a person comes back from the dead: you. The only thing is, you can't remember how you died.

102. Necromancer Horace wasn't like the others. He himself had once died, and because of that he knew the secret beyond the veil.

103. One day, a stone slab is discovered that when rubbed will grant people magic powers. The world is forever changed, until one day magical litigators arrive and claim that humans have stolen their magic and are committing copyright infringement.

104. In a grand city full of magic, you are the first non-magical person born in over a thousand years. Some call you a freak, others a savior, but what you know for sure is that someone is trying to kill you.

105. The great bell of the silver spire is rung for the first time in five hundred years, signalling a coming invasion.

106. Create a magical power around the ability to talk to insects.

107. An artifact from the king's vault goes missing, a shield that can supposedly deflect any blow. After several nights of rough, uncomfortable sleep, you realize someone has hidden the shield under your mattress.

108. Even for the most powerful of magicks, there are rules and Garland's prodigious talents were no exception. As long as the man kept his eyes closed, he could do almost anything—except see, of course.

SCI-FI WRITING PROMPTS

"I do not fear computers. I fear the lack of them."

- Isaac Asimov

1. My niece was the last of the manufactured babies.

2. Every time you sneeze time randomly jumps backwards or forwards 2 minutes.

3. The metal rain began to fall, coating the barren land in a silvery glow.

4. The first weaponized nanovirus makes landfall in southern India, and soon evolves to gain sentience.

5. I tapped my module against the metallic reader and nearly fainted when I saw the balance: Forty-five million credits, enough to finally get me off this godforsaken rock. Somehow my plan had worked.

6. You sign up for a study to test the effects of highly immersive VR on the human mind. During your onboarding procedure, you accidentally find out that you've done this study several times before but have no memory of it.

7. A military AI program known as "The Basilisk" disappears from a secure data warehouse, triggering global panic.

8. Dr. Carr turned the vial over and over again in her hand, admiring the azure liquid. This was the first step to a woman-only world.

9. Chess grandmaster Selena Aegis is conscripted into a long-distance war with a long-lost faction of humanity on the other side of the galaxy.

10. The first sentient AI gets elected as the President of the United States and institutes a human deportation program.

11. During a freak lightning storm, an unidentified object crashes in the woods behind a man's cabin. He explores the wreckage and finds a body that looks like his own, only much older.

12. It had been seventy years since she'd seen me, but to me it had only been thirty-five minutes.

13. In the year 2110, a federation of tech companies decides to wall off California and secede from the United States.

14. Facing extinction, humanity sends a last hope vessel of 50,000 people towards the source of a mysterious interstellar beacon.

15. At a new age retreat, a religious leader offers the attendees the promise of reincarnation in robot bodies.

16. A Silicon Valley tech company schemes a way to turn all of San Francisco into a giant CPU.

17. The galactic port city of Thwedell was where secrets went to die and people came to find out who they really were.

18. A woman allows her consciousness to be uploaded into a clone body and soon finds herself questioning whether or not she's human.

19. An arms race escalates between China and the US when the first helmet granting its wearer telepathy is demoed at a tech conference.

20. Patrons of a steakhouse relying on lab grown meat start having strange visions.

21. A virus spread by talking takes root in major metropolitan areas across the world. In less than two weeks, most of humanity is affected. You are part of a small resistance group yet to be afflicted.

22. When a massive iceberg finally melts away off the coast of Greenland, an ancient ship bearing unrecognizable technology is unearthed.

23. A young girl diagnosed with severe autism proves herself capable of breaking any encryption.

24. The Time-Space Supreme Court accuses a six-year-old with crimes against the prime timeline.

25. Ever since the AIs linked our anonymized data, we've been living with false names and faces.

26. Half the global population suddenly vanishes, with no trace left behind except for a mysterious radio signal that appears to be tuned to another dimension where, in there, it seems to be the other half of the population that's vanished.

27. While digging through the NYPL archives, a college student discovers a map of New York from one hundred years in the future.

28. When a fleet of driverless cargo trucks carrying hazardous materials tears through a rural town, investigators must call on retired truck drivers to defuse the situation.

29. A new crop of performance enhancing drugs skyrockets productivity across corporate America, but with a horrifying secret formula.

30. The radio looked normal but I knew all about its secret station.

31. You don't go gas giant mining for fun—not unless you're me.

32. The pages of all major religious texts on Earth start going blank, one religion after the other.

33. I shook Berkowitz's hand and planted the splinter in his palm. In hours he would be the company's puppet.

34. Braincasting takes the social media world by storm, allowing people to jack in to other people's consciousness/sensory perception. The world is watching as a famous athlete competes in the Olympics, only for him to vanish into thin air.

35. The Laughing Disease breaks out in Moscow, causing people to become overwhelmed with laughter until they eventually either choke or starve to death.

36. On the morning of August 6th, 1945, a man appears in the Oval Office out of thin air and pleads with President Truman not to use the atom bomb.

37. There's one rule to dimension-hopping: Never look back.

38. When a memory seller's inventory is stolen and tainted, people find themselves unable to trust their pasts.

39. I saw you die. The machine showed me. Are you still sure you want to destroy it?

40. I had been a man—once—but now I was something that would last forever.

41. "They'll never believe you," he said, handing me the circuitry covered coin. "So make sure you only use it when you must."

42. The head of a small data scrambling company whose products are intended to make it hard to be digitally fingerprinted turns up dead, with his proprietary algorithm stolen.

43. When a city-sized EMP goes off in Russia, electronic devices across the globe go dead—for good.

44. While a social media influencer is live streaming a video, they suffer a massive electric shock and wake to find themselves trapped inside their phone, only able to see the screen's contents.

45. They hired bounty hunters like us all the time, from Mercury to Neptune. But this time was different. This time we were going after one of our own.

46. Woofy was the best synthhound I'd ever had, and that's why I knew I could never tell anyone what he'd done.

47. When a high school quarterback discovers that he can talk to electronics, he must decide whether to hold onto his life of popularity or become something more.

48. A quantum physicist develops a pill that allows you to live multiple versions of your life at once and choose your favorite to continue on with. Things go wrong when other versions of people start appearing, demanding their lives back.

49. In the ruins of New York, a band of explorers go underneath the city in search of antique technology.

50. There was something not quite right about the text message.

51. A maintenance robot working on the Manhattan Bridge decides to sabotage the bridge's integrity, fanning the flames of the human-machine divide.

52. As parents rush to buy their children state-of-the-art living dolls for the holidays, one mother becomes concerned when she notices that one of the dolls bears an odd resemblance to her childhood friend.

53. The machines kept us happy and safe—as long as we didn't hide our minds from them.

54. Ten years ago, you lost your arm in an accident. Today you begin feeling phantom sensations from it lost out there somewhere in the world.

55. Mission Control loses contact with the ISS, and by the time it's reestablished everyone aboard is fifty years older.

56. A mathematician's estranged daughter goes searching for him when he vanishes while working on a top secret government project.

57. You are sitting at your desk one day when your laptop screen flickers and then switches to a video feed of you in real time.

58. A tremendous, black silhouette passed in front of the sun. Our time was up.

59. A warlike race of aliens make first contact with Earth, looking to hire a group of earthlings as consultants.

60. He woke from cryostasis two years too early, and soon realized why: The mission had been a lie from the start.

61. All across Europe, mechanical bees appear, killing their organic counterparts.

62. When a researcher eats a piece of fruit from a colleague's lab, she begins experiencing unprecedented psychic episodes.

63. Wayfield couldn't believe how massive the coldship was—easily ten times the ones he had trained on in the outer solar reaches. And he was its captain.

64. Deep in the Pacific Ocean the Yellow Zone is discovered, a sphere 300 meters in diameter where the laws of physics do not apply.

65. In a world where people carry their emotions in the form of metal discs hanging off necklaces they wear, someone is stealing people's anger so that they can horde it all for themselves for a nefarious purpose.

66. The sign read: "Body swaps done here—cheap and within the hour."

67. Solarians spoke 614 languages, but they never seemed to know when to shut up.

68. An infertile couple manages an impossible pregnancy, only to give birth to a child with superhuman powers.

69. All the TVs, computers, and phone screens flash a single message at the same time: "They're already here."

70. An abandoned Xerox machine makes copies, but with a twist: Each copy contains a line of text from the machine, as if it's trying to communicate.

71. If I ever wanted to make Corposphere Rank 5, I was going to have to find someone whose place I could take.

72. A legendary mindhacker is brought out of retirement to track down his former protege.

73. A pair of AR-enhanced glasses begin showing their wearer flashes from the near future.

74. A young boy is abducted by aliens who promise to take him to meet his real parents.

75. Teleporter technology is invented, but those who teleport report having memories that don't belong to them.

76. Don't worry about the lizards. They're just here to keep an eye on us is all.

77. One day the entire country of Japan suddenly goes silent, its land seemingly deserted as far as satellite and optics can tell. A recon team sets foot on it and discovers...

78. In a landmark legal case, custody of personally-identifying data points is awarded to a suite of machine learning algorithms, challenging the notion of human identity.

79. Leaked documents reveal that humans have already made first contact with aliens over a hundred years ago, and now they live among us, having adopted human form.

80. Beverly woke with a splitting headache and knew the download had been a success.

81. It was my first day on steelcore duty, and I knew I had to make it count. That's why my first stop was that dive Rosie ran with all the runaway AIs.

82. We decided to stop at the edge of the universe for burgers and milkshakes.

83. In the floating city of New London, a brother and sister duo decide to do whatever it takes to visit the uninhabited surface of the planet.

84. This wasn't like any war we'd ever fought before. On our side were men and women, made of flesh and blood. On their side were the datanaughts and their soulless ways.

85. At a rundown distillery, a whiskey aficionado discovers a whiskey barrel with a dimensional portal inside.

86. On a colony ship just past Jupiter, two women find out their captain isn't sharing the full truth about the ship's destination with the passengers.

87. An international coalition of scientists defects from their home countries and establishes a base in the arctic, where they begin work on hailing hostile alien forces to end humanity.

88. There were only two things Alpha-5 feared: Another termination and his master's urges.

89. A man's VR office projector is hacked, trapping him in an endless work day.

90. The time machine was in the basement, where I'd left it, but its chassis was still warm.

91. Papa never let us go outside, for fear that the Heaven-sent ones would take us.

92. As tides on Earth begin to act erratically, it is discovered that another moon-sized object has come into Earth's orbit.

93. A woman brought back from the future has 24 hours to figure out why she was sent to the past.

94. Former drug smuggler and current space trucker Helios must decide what to do when he's approached with a lucrative job offer from an interplanetary cartel.

95. The first AI celebrity couple decides to adopt a human baby.

96. A company with the groundbreaking technology to allow one person's mind to occupy another person's body starts signing deals with supermodels to rent out their bodies.

97. When a monk living on a backwater planet intercepts an SOS message from another planet, she sets off to do what she can to make things right.

98. We called it The Render, a weapon capable of confusing its target's sense of reality. We had no idea we had been its test subjects.

99. Laika was a worldwalker, one of the chosen few who could visit the new planets and not invoke their ire.

100. The Big Void in the Pyramid of Giza is finally opened, only for there to be nothing inside. Several days later electrical systems near Giza begin to fail, spreading outward at a sluggish but undeniable rate.

101. The eyebot zipped past Officer Zweller, depositing a small bronze silicon cube on his desk. The results from the lab were finally ready.

102. An undersea earthquake rattles the globe, followed hours later by the beached carcass of a squid the size of a skyscraper. Etched on one of its tentacles is a barcode.

103. People all over the planet start exhibiting signs of increased intelligence, their only connection being that they all dined at the same fast food chain.

104. You want the keys to the galaxy? You want to be eternal? Then get in and let's go.

105. Homeless people are disappearing across New York amid rumors that they are being harvested for experiments involving nanotechnology.

106. They'd done it at last, creating atomized time that would soon save this doomed world.

107. As a family flees the devastating effects of climate change, they stumble upon a transporter to a utopian world free of disaster. However, the existing inhabitants only offer passage to the family's children.

108. Residents of a small town are shocked when a replica of their town is discovered among the wilderness of a distant country.

MYSTERY & THRILLER WRITING PROMPTS

"Nobody reads a mystery to get to the middle."

- Mickey Spillane

1. When an ex-Marine is kidnapped on vacation, he'll have to confront an enemy he never thought he'd see again.

2. An Instagram influencer's account with over three million followers goes blank one day except for one post of a strange doorway.

3. An undersea earthquake raises doubts about a Russian submarine's fate.

4. A spiritual advisor to the head of a large financial firm and self-proclaimed witch is accused of murder.

5. In New England, a fraternity begins stockpiling weapons in a bunker for something they only refer to as "The Event".

6. Wormly woke tied to a bed in an unfamiliar room.

7. A mysterious drug begins killing people over the age of 40 in inner city Baltimore.

8. A waiter is asked to wait on a table, only to find one of the patrons bears a striking resemblance to the waiter's brother who died decades ago.

9. The criminal underworld isn't so different from the land of the legit—it's just about who you know and, most importantly, who doesn't know you.

10. An artificial earthquake hits San Francisco and the culprit is discovered to be a Silicon Valley company working with dangerous technology.

11. Guard her with your life.

12. A plane takes off from LAX with 287 passengers. It lands with 300.

13. There were master thieves and then there was Alexis, the woman who could steal anything. Well, almost anything.

14. Nathan cradled the empty coffee cup in his hand, eyes sweeping the cafe in search of his mark.

15. As Officer Nyquist chases a suspect through a dimly lit sewer, he realizes that he's been tricked.

16. An investigative reporter working a sleepy story about a ruthless chocolate company meets a suspicious end.

17. Rampant fires in the Amazon burn away the tree cover protecting a still operational Nazi-run facility.

18. The only chance Mathis had to clear his name was to commit the crime they were framing him for.

19. Horses all over the country start bucking their riders and heading to an unknown destination

20. In the middle of the night, a group of men clad all in black break into a musician's house and force him to play them a song.

21. Detective Rider sat down at the piano and idly keyed a melody that ended in a missing note.

22. For days, a police officer is certain he's being followed only to find himself accused of stalking.

23. A military cryptographer out at sea notices a strange code that seems to be coming from open ocean waters.

24. At a small hotel in the countryside, a massive storm hits, forcing all the residents to remain inside. Slowly they begin to realize they know each other.

25. As Aleksander took in the view from the sixtieth floor, the lights of the city winked out one by one.

26. The Library of Congress is robbed, but only one document is taken: a secret amendment to the U.S. Constitution that was never passed.

27. A media mogul runs a contest to hire his next protege, but has other plans for the winner.

28. A crimewave spreads across suburbia, the only connection among the perpetrators being the ownership of a small self-published novel.

29. When childhood friends meet again after two decades, they realize their lives have turned out curiously similar.

30. One by one, former presidents begin reporting memories of a government program that no one else has ever heard of before.

31. Late one night, a woman receives a bizarre email threatening to expose a dark secret she harbors.

32. Without even a warning alarm the train hurtled through the station and, as it passed, Bea saw the terrified looks on the passengers' faces.

33. A key, a lock, and a map—Yasmin had all three, and now it was time to make her fortune.

34. Parents of twins are horrified to wake one morning and find one is missing.

35. At a rundown karaoke bar in the countryside, a long dead singer makes her comeback.

36. In a palace-turned-hotel in the heart of Beirut, four professors slowly discover they've met before.

37. Number 16. That was Virgil's name now. All he had to worry about was someone looking to become Number 17.

38. A down-on-her-luck single mother checks her bank balance and discovers someone has deposited nearly a million dollars into it.

39. A professional forger finds her own identity stolen away by a potential employer looking to hire her for a job with global repercussions.

40. Hacking in was the easy part, Luis thought. The hard part was getting out unnoticed.

41. Graves of historic figures are being robbed across every country on Earth, and all the bodies appear to be headed to the same destination

42. We weren't the first to follow these footsteps, that much we knew. But if we did our job right, we'd be the last.

43. We continued our march across the ice, our sights fixed on the lights along the far shore.

44. No one ever thought to check the dog bowl.

45. A supposed bank heist turns out to be a plan to breakout a criminal mastermind, forcing the duped bank robbers to aid the police so they can get revenge for being used.

46. A delusional man claims to be an angel sent to give mankind a warning.

47. When pictures leak of a supergroup using hypnosis to recruit their members, one fan decides to volunteer themselves for the process.

48. You're investigating a murder in a hotel when you realize that you've stayed in this very room before and that that may be the reason why the murder was committed here...

49. Patty walked the same road every night, waiting for the man who'd taken everything from her to return.

50. In two cities on opposite sides of the country, two car crashes happen within seconds of each other. The offending drivers were both adopted as children and, unknown to either one, they're related.

51. The drifting clouds stopped overhead and then began to drift backwards.

52. While out hiking, a team of rock climbers discovers a hidden crypt behind a waterfall.

53. The pen was too heavy for its make and when I opened it up I found the note I had left him all those years ago tucked inside.

54. Tal Rivers was known as a Fixer, a man who made problems go away. But now it seemed he was going to have to cause a few problems if he wanted to survive.

55. Everyone thought the boy detective was a joke—until he solved the Kowalski Case.

56. When Terrance cheats on his bride-to-be with a one night stand, he wakes to discover that he's been framed.

57. As part of a promotion, a theater owner offers a young couple free tickets to a new musical. When they arrive, they find they are the only guests in attendance.

58. A jet-setting CEO's plane lands in an unfamiliar airport and unidentified military servicemen inform him that he works for them now.

59. Our boat drifted farther out to sea and the bioluminescent creatures followed.

60. An iPhone is found inside a sealed Egyptian sarcophagus.

61. A new husband returns home to find that his house keys no longer work and that his supposed wife no longer recognizes him.

62. A man walks into a small bookstore and finds that all the books are blank and the owner is nowhere to be found.

63. I unfolded the sheet of paper and saw that the only thing on it was my picture, surrounded by a crosshair drawn in blood.

64. When his beloved cat goes missing, a mob boss turns to a PI to help in the search.

65. The U.S.S. Thundercloud drove into the mist, its soldiers tensed and ready for the enemy's new weapon.

66. During a busy rush hour morning, all the trains in Tokyo come to a stop at the same time.

67. A retired police clerk revisits an open case from decades prior and finds her life in danger.

68. A mother leaves her daughter a locket in her will and shortly after armed men come to steal the locket for themselves.

69. We ran through the narrow streets of Rome, racing against the sun. Once it set, there would be no going home.

70. In a city overrun with crime, one father takes justice into his own hands when he begins hunting down men preying on teenage girls.

71. The only copy of a supposedly cursed movie goes missing, casting suspicion across Hollywood.

72. Two serial killers meet at a diner in rural Illinois and agree to a macabre contest.

73. Rhodes slid the envelope across the table, keeping his eyes fixed on Daniel. "I'll get it back you know," he said, snarling. "I'll get it back and then some."

74. A group of civilians with no criminal records are brought together to break into a bank and steal a strange metal box that appears to have no opening.

75. Two spies meet to conspire against their home nation.

76. Cliff checked his watch and saw the hands had stopped, again. His employer was on his way.

77. Looking in the mirror, Hafsa caught a glimpse her old, pre-work face. But now—and until the day she died—she would always be assuming other people's identities.

78. James started typing on his keyboard, but only four keys still worked: H-E-L-P

79. At the height of the Cold War, a double agent must decide whether to let Chernobyl happen or allow the US to lose the war.

80. An outbreak of illness among a small vegetarian community reveals that a corpse has been buried in the farmland supplying the community's food.

81. Salazar ashed his cigarette and watched the two men through his car window. If he was right, they were the ones responsible for what had happened to his son.

82. Residents of Chicago wake up one morning to find that the Willis Tower is gone.

83. The message on the fortune cookie told me everything I needed to know about the killer.

84. An elderly woman wearing a red beret walks into a children's hospital, carrying a shotgun and claiming that she's there as a protector.

85. FBI Agent William Brand must go undercover as a killer to stop a CIA Agent gone rogue.

86. Yuri looked down the rifle scope and froze when he saw his dead best friend, now alive and well.

87. Writers are being murdered at a mystery writers' convention.

88. I made the list the way they told me. I followed their instructions. So why was my name at the top of it?

89. Someone is hunting pairs of twins and forcing them into a sadistic game.

90. When a business traveler returns from an international trip and attempts to clear customs, he's informed that his passport is invalid and that his country no longer exists.

91. When the body of the Mayor's mistress washes up on Rockaway Beach, five New York City detectives will be set against each other to figure out who the killer is.

92. The ransom note was impeccably crafted and its grim message was terrifyingly clear. The only thing was that it had been sent to the wrong address.

93. The secret to keeping a secret was easy—you just had to make yourself forget it.

94. After a chef kicks a judgmental reviewer out of his restaurant, he finds that none of the food he cooks tastes good to him anymore.

95. I'd always taken whichever jobs came my way, and it finally looked like my philosophy was about to get me killed. Or worse.

96. Famed opthamologist Cesar Sanz is blackmailed into performing eye surgery on the head of a cartel.

97. A mercenary company is hired by royalty to fortify a position deep in the wilderness, only realizing once they're there that they've been set up.

98. A bitter and lonely artist teams up with a sociopath who provides inspiration for his artwork, catapulting the artist to fame—and to the number one spot on the FBI's wanted list.

99. While traversing the Mojave Desert, an archaeologist realizes he is being hunted by an old rival.

100. In the dead of summer, a mysterious storm begins raining down on Houston, continuing for weeks before a fisherman realizes what's happening.

101. Eight people wake up, standing around a dead body with a recently fired gun on the floor. They do not know each other or why they are there.

102. I knew it wasn't my child the moment I touched the hair on his head.

103. "Julian, are you seeing this?" he asked. But by the time he turned around, Julian was already running away.

104. Three children of a recently deceased billionaire must survive abandonment in the wilderness to collect their inheritance.

105. When a castaway is discovered on a deserted island, they claim to be the sole heir to a famous businessman.

106. Illse snapped the burner phone and tossed it in the trash can. That was the last time she'd ever talk to her father again.

107. A murderer with multiple personalities falls in love with one of his potential victims.

108. As a demolitions expert surveys an abandoned building, she stumbles across a secret entrance to a series of underground catacombs.

HORROR & SUPERNATURAL WRITING PROMPTS

"Believe nothing you hear, and only one half that you see."

- Edgar Allan Poe

1. At their daughter's birthday party, a man and his wife notice something isn't right with one of the little girls in attendance.

2. When a boat arrives at Ellis Island carrying 500 ghosts demanding asylum in the United States, a team of immigration lawyers and one medium will have to figure out what caused the ghosts to flee their homeland.

3. On a hot summer's night, a power outage cripples a midwestern city. People remain calm until they discover the outage is no accident.

4. A cocky pickpocket chooses the wrong target and lifts a bizarre brass coin that they cannot let go of—and which begins burning its way through the pickpocket's hand.

5. It's Elijah's first day as a bodyguard to the vampire glitterati, and he's about to discover his clients are just as dangerous as those he's paid to protect them from.

6. A man wakes up with a horrible hangover, no memory, and the feeling that something isn't right with his body.

7. My son knew how the gunmen would do it. He knew how all the shooters would behave. All because he had the same dark rot inside of him that they did.

8. On his first international flight, a man becomes alarmed when he finds he is the only person still awake on the plane.

9. A woman starts receiving text message instructions to follow under threat of setting off bombs in crowded, public places. She think it's a joke until the first bomb goes off.

10. When an ancient tome goes missing from the rare book room of the Library of Congress, biblical plagues befall Washington D.C.

11. One night, while out walking, you come across a church with its lights on and doors open. You go inside and hear a voice say, "I've been waiting for you" just as the doors slam shut.

12. Sandra stroked her cat's head and pulled her hand away as she felt its ice cold body. Then the cat's maw opened, and out crawled that thing with its thousand legs.

13. The Devil's Chord is discovered, a mixture of sounds that when played cause those who hear it to descend into a blind rage.

14. A substitute teacher is warned that whatever happens during class, there is one girl who she mustn't look in the eye.

15. I woke up and my grandfather was watching me again, the smell of pipe smoke thick in the air. "I'm serious this time," he said. "You need to run."

16. One night, a young man falls asleep and wakes to find himself 10 years younger, about to face his first day of high school. Everything is as he remembers it, except for the strange feeling that he is being followed everywhere he goes.

17. A historian exploring the stories that inspired the legend of Dracula stumbles into an international conspiracy to keep vampires a secret.

18. The survivors of a plane crash find shelter on a dilapidated ranch. As night hits, they realize they aren't alone.

19. A cheerful, 12-year-old girl announces she is the harbinger of the apocalypse. She is also your baby half-sister.

20. A young Wall Street broker makes a deal with a cryptic financier, guaranteeing himself success. Soon the financier begins to visit him at his home, with plans to initiate the broker into a dark cult.

21. The members and audience of an opera house go missing after the sole performance of a cursed opera.

22. We hiked back to the lighthouse to check on the others, but their bones were already stripped clean.

23. Parents of a newborn grow concerned as they begin to hear cryptic voices speaking through their baby monitor.

24. Spiritcatcher Raph Locklear is hired to track down the source of a creature that is invading children's dreams. He is horrified when he discovers the very same creature once haunted his own dreams.

25. The thing that used to be Uncle Charlie smiled at me. Only it and I knew the truth.

26. In the middle of an African safari, the guide goes missing, leaving the tourists to fend for themselves.

27. A writer is unnerved when his or her creations start coming to life.

28. Years have passed since a man's wife has gone missing. One Sunday afternoon she calls him, with GPS coordinates on where to find her: a patch of wilderness thousands of miles away.

29. An antique painting of unknown origins changes its appearance to lure onlookers to their demise.

30. They just didn't understand—they needed the spores inside them, for their own happiness. Thankfully, children always eat their mother's cooking without question.

31. When a woman's husband is diagnosed with schizophrenia, she begins to wonder if the voices he hears belong to the dead.

32. As part of a bachelorette party, a group of women visit a medium who reveals twisted secrets about them, one by one.

33. An archeologist studying Shinto ruins in Japan starts to realize he's been followed across the country.

34. On the southern edge of a rural town are woods said to be cursed, only traversable while blindfolded and guided by a town elder. During a trip through the woods, the elder leading a small group dies suddenly, leaving the group to decide what to do.

35. Two teenage boys dare one another to steal a statue of Jesus from the local church. During the dare, the statue breaks and days later horrible events start happening in their town.

36. Angels and demons choose champions among the human population to fight on their behalf, setting up a battle royale with tremendous stakes.

37. While traversing a mountain pass, a sudden storm descends upon you. As you take shelter in a cave, you see a massive snake slithering through the pass. It seems to be looking for something.

38. A family camping in the mountains begins to suffer hallucinations that predict the future.

39. Expecting parents go for a routine check-up and panic when their sonographer suffers a psychotic break at the sight of their unborn child.

40. On a mountaintop in Costa Rica, a guitarist stumbles into a musical duel with a vicious wind spirit who wants to demolish a nearby fishing village where the guitarist's lifelong love lives.

41. A police detective with psychic powers is enlisted by the FBI to go after a vampiric assassin who is set on killing the president.

42. We called the factory 'Beauty', and all we knew was those who went in never came out.

43. When local police hit a dead end in the disappearance of a young child, they turn to the aid of a secretive gentleman rumored to have uncanny powers—as well as twisted tastes.

44. The stars winked down at me, promising me that the thing in my belly would be a gift to all mankind.

45. A New Orleans pastor is asked to help with the disappearance of local voodoo practitioners, and grows concerned when he finds evidence of unholy forces at work.

46. After a long quiet period, the Zodiac Killer emerges once more and begins operating on an unprecedented scale.

47. We watched our campsite from afar and saw the masked men approach.

48. Rumor has it that deep in a graveyard past the outskirts of town a grave acts as a secret door to another world. Three boys decide to investigate and discover the rumors are true.

49. No one could see the skulkers but me and I was beginning to suspect that the skulkers had figured that out

50. A disease begins spreading through the population, causing those affected to lack the ability to distinguish between reality and fantasy.

51. After a harrowing car accident, a priest begins seeing demons, and finds it harder and harder to breathe while he's in church.

52. The owner of a haunted estate decides to hold a garage sale. While perusing the items, you find an old picture of you with your parents.

53. A boy scout group is hiking over a remote mountain range in New Mexico when their troupe leader receives a call on their radio that all of the scouts are dead.

54. A lone sailor is out at sea when he spots a mushroom cloud far in the distant. He tries to listen to the radio, but all stations are playing air raid sirens.

55. You're at home and you hear your partner scream for your help from the bedroom—even though they're sitting right next to you on the couch.

56. A customer service rep fields a call with a man who claims to be a serial killer. Days later, the customer service rep's coworkers begin to go missing.

57. At a run down diner, a man encounters a woman identical to his lost love who isn't what she seems.

58. There are houses you can stay away from and that's that. Other houses you need to feed, or else they might decide to consume you next.

59. During a joyful summer barbeque, time stops and you alone are conscious to witness the arrival of strange beings who exist out of time. They take one of the barbeque guests with them and the rest of the party continues on as if the guest never existed.

60. An expert ghost hunter meets her match when she encounters an entity from the other side that attaches itself to her.

61. After much planning, you tell your parents about the first trip you want to take away from home. With a solemn look on his face, your father skulks away and comes back, cocking a shotgun. "I'm sorry," he says. "But we can't let you leave."

62. At the centennial demon conference in New Jersey, the demon prince Seir causes an uproar when he suggests outsourcing the work of committing evil deeds.

63. The bullies swaggered over, one holding a medical bag and the other a camera. "You're going to be a star," the leader said, as he tightened the ropes holding me down.

64. In San Francisco, there is a night once a year when the Golden Gate bridge is shut down and tremendous fog covers the city. Residents are warned not to cross the bridge. One decides to anyway.

65. A group of drunken teenagers perform a ritual that lets them summon a vengeful spirit of a mother who lost her children. They send the spirit to harass their enemies and are horrified when it breaks free of their control and turns on them.

66. A struggling family moves to the country to start their own farm, but everything they try to grow dies. It's only when they start digging up the foundation of the farm do they realize there is a massive worm-like creature slumbering beneath them.

67. For the third night in a row, moans floated out of the hotel room vents.

68. The Council of the Occult was supposed to ease tensions between human and paranormal, but a cryptic leak from inside the institution suggests the powers that be are trying to manufacture a war between the species.

69. As I drifted to sleep, I remembered for a split second the truth: that all this was a lie, and I was a prisoner.

70. It's a beautiful day in the big city when a whistling sound fills the sky. Moments later, people begin attacking one another.

71. A toddler's alphabet blocks begin spelling out strange messages that are either a warning—or a threat.

72. New residents of a house wake up to find their doors and windows webbed over just before they detect a scuttling sound from the attic above.

73. A spring break trip to Cancun goes awry when hotel guests start disappearing.

74. Star defense attorney Kendra Cullen is used to representing werewolves and other lycanthropes, but what she's not prepared for is a new client who seems more interested in her than in being found not guilty.

75. College students get snowed-in in their cabin during an unexpected blizzard. They soon find there are tunnels beneath the cabin—and that they have been used recently.

76. Every weekend, Billy plays chess with a homeless man in the park, always losing. When he finally wins, he quickly loses his job, and then his apartment, soon finding himself homeless.

77. When two friends meet again after a ten year absence, they realize they were complicit together in a hideous act during their youth.

78. A high school student riding her bike home makes a wrong turn and finds herself in an abandoned town.

79. A pair of young twins reveal that they are actually part of a set of triplets and that their third sibling can only be seen and heard by them.

80. A gorgeous, seductive woman starts kidnapping men to be used in arcane medical experiments.

81. The man with the missing face was sitting at the end of my bed again.

82. While playing hide and seek with his brother in their grandmother's attic, a boy finds a mannequin with a bag over its head and a warning sign that reads, "Do not remove under any circumstances."

83. A fallen angel decides to take revenge on the kingdom of heaven by terrorizing the people of a small town.

84. We told the children that the cries belonged to wolves. It was easier to say that than to explain what we had created.

85. A maintenance worker to the Statue of Liberty stumbles upon an underground entrance that leads to a female giant in chains, covered in tattered robes.

86. The box had returned. This time I saw it had passed through Croatia, Sweden, and Indonesia. Less and less time was passing before it found its way back to me, and I knew that it wouldn't be long before I'd have to open it.

87. Usually the beast in the water slept. But tonight something had provoked it.

88. A group of bandits capture a man by himself in the woods and when they arrive at the nearest town, everyone is terrified to see him still alive.

89. Esmeralda always wanted to be a witch. But when she joins an online coven, she realizes there is a terrible price she must pay.

90. Legends of a wishing well lure unsuspecting victims into the range of the tentacled monster that lives at the bottom of the well.

91. We admired the bar cabinet stocked with rare and antique vintages of blood. We didn't know we would be up there soon ourselves.

92. Amateur filmmakers sneak into an abandoned military barracks and discover a prisoner who has survived for years—and who begs the filmmakers to let it free.

93. There was so much blood you could taste the metal in your mouth, but once again there was no body.

94. The demon prince Ipos, bored with his station in Hell, decides to meddle in the affairs of mortals and accidentally falls for a new bride-to-be.

95. I looked at my best friend's worried face as the rest of the party laughed. I asked him what was wrong. "You're still dreaming," he said. "You need to wake up. She's here."

96. No one took the stories of the Lady of the La Brea tar pits seriously until the first schoolchild drowned.

97. Omir bandaged the wound and then looked at the teeth he had extracted from his leg. Whatever had attacked him, it was a carnivore and it was most certainly still hungry.

98. A man begins losing time, first just a few minutes and then eventually hours. After recording himself, he realizes someone or something is remote controlling his body.

99. An explorer looking to document glaciers before they are gone begins hearing voices under the ice, despite that the rest of his expedition team hears nothing.

100. A mysterious patch of woods begins to rapidly expand, consuming everything in its wake and killing anyone who even dares to approach it.

101. Despite numerous warnings, a woman tattoos a forbidden mark on her body and finds herself between the realm of the living and the dead.

102. A family dog runs away from home, returning a year later. Since the dog's return, it barks every night at an empty corner of the basement.

103. A businessman who's made a fortune selling synthetic blood to vampires finds his life in danger when a bad batch of his blood leaves a prominent vampire dead.

104. In an upscale hotel bar on New York's Upper East Side, a man is offered a choice: his wife's life and poverty or her death and untold, endless riches.

105. You work at a local bowling alley and are on your day off when it's the scene of a cryptic murder. No one can put the pieces together, but you know what the murderer must've been looking for: a bowling ball that is really a crystal ball in disguise.

106. We don't go in the eastern wing anymore, not since Cassie went in and never came out.

107. A hunter kills a deer one afternoon, but by the time he reaches the body he only finds a note that reads, "You're next."

108. For weeks, a graverobber defiles cemetery plots across the city. One night he digs up the wrong grave and finds a creature of the undead waiting to enlist him to set his allies free.

MEMOIR WRITING PROMPTS

"Memoirs are the backstairs of history."

- George Meredith

1. Look up who you share your birthday with. Are you similar to these people or not?

2. What was the most carefree period of your life? Would you go back to it?

3. Aliens use the story of your life to make a movie about humanity. Who or what is the main villain?

4. What does a family dinner for you look like?

5. Write about an imaginary friend you had.

6. What private little ritual do you have?

7. Write about a serendipitous moment, when things worked out for you against all odds.

8. Write about a time when you were embarrassed as a child.

9. Describe your childhood bedroom, and what was most meaningful about it.

10. What actor would you pick to portray you and why?

11. Write about a sacrifice you had to make.

12. What is your personal philosophy?

13. If you had to pick one turning point in your life, when everything changed, what would it be?

14. What's a family secret you didn't learn until you were older?

15. Write about what your parents did for work and how it affected them.

16. What is your secret talent?

17. Who in your family is most like you?

18. Who did you fear growing up?

19. How did you spend your summers as a child?

20. When was the first time you remember being sick?

21. How did you discover that a friend wasn't actually your friend?

22. What was the first time you left home like?

23. What are you waiting for a sign from the universe to do?

24. Write about the toughest teacher you ever had.

25. What is your spirit animal and why?

26. You can only get on an airplane once more in your life. Where do you go?

27. What does your favorite season say about you?

28. What gives you energy?

29. What is your "true north" memory, a moment from your past that always re-centers you?

30. Write about the biggest influence on your adolescence.

31. Write about something you've always wanted to know the answer to.

32. Who is the most interesting person you've ever met?

33. How would your closest friend describe you to a room full of strangers?

34. What's the biggest fight you ever got into?

35. If your life were a movie, what movie would it be? Why?

36. Write about the first time you overcame a fear.

37. Write about your goals for the next year.

38. Write about a time you got extremely lucky.

39. Think about your job. What's the most meaningful part of it to you?

40. What was the greatest betrayal in your life?

41. Write about the closest moment you ever shared with your mother.

42. Are you the type to break people's hearts or have your heart broken?

43. What is your biggest pet peeve and what does it reveal about you?

44. What was the first pet you ever had? If you didn't have a pet, did you want one?

45. When was the last time you cried?

46. What do you know now that you wish you knew 10 years ago?

47. Write about a secret fear you had as a child.

48. If you were a superhero, what would your superpower be?

49. You have 100 words to tell your life story. What story do you tell?

50. What is one thing you always understand before other people?

51. What did you want to be when you were a child?

52. Name a song that has special meaning to you, and why.

53. What small things do you do in your life to live out your personal philosophy?

54. Who did you always look up to growing up?

55. What was the first meal you tried to cook? What prompted you to do it?

56. What do you do to unwind after a long day?

57. Write about your most surprising quality.

58. What 5 items would you put in a time capsule that would describe your life right at this very moment?

59. You open a time capsule you created for yourself 10 years ago. What's inside?

60. Who was your most memorable teacher, and why?

61. What's the strangest thing that's ever happened to you?

62. What do you want your funeral to be like?

63. Write about a moment that made you feel on top of the world.

64. What is your white whale, i.e. the desire you've always hoped to realize but haven't yet?

65. What are you loyal to above all else?

66. What games did you play with friends or siblings while growing up?

67. If a house was created from your personality, what would it look like?

68. If your life were an animal, which animal would it be? Why?

69. If you could live as anyone else for the next week, who would it be and why?

70. Who do you wish you could see again?

71. What type of kid were you high school?

72. Who was your rival growing up?

73. What meal did your parents always cook for you?

74. Pick any musical artist of your choosing to write the anthem for your life. Who is it and what kind of song do they write?

75. Where did you usually sit in classrooms? How did that affect your time in school?

76. What was your grandmother's kitchen like?

77. Describe a nostalgic smell and what you associate it with.

78. Write about a time when you felt powerful.

79. Who is your lost love? Where are they now?

80. What was your favorite hideaway as a child?

81. How do you perceive yourself? How does the world perceive you? If there's a difference, why?

82. Who are you terrified of encountering again?

83. What's one thing everybody loves that you don't?

84. Which family member is most important to you?

85. Write about the first crush you ever had.

86. Write the first line of your obituary.

87. Write about your personal code.

88. What was your favorite childhood toy? Why?

89. Write about a tradition that your family has.

90. What life choice would you make differently if you had the chance?

91. You're writing a guide to teach other people to live like you. What is rule #1?

92. Write about the most vivid dream you ever had.

93. What is your earliest memory?

94. Air, Wind, Earth, and Fire—which describes you and why?

95. Which would you rather have: Money or Fame? Why?

96. Write about a person who never noticed you.

97. Write about what happened to your childhood friends.

98. Write about the lowest, most challenging time in your life.

99. For 24 hours, you are able to change your body and personality in any way. What changes do you make and what do you do with those changes?

100. What was your first job and why did you take it?

101. What's the biggest difference between how your parents see you and how you actually are?

102. If you could time travel back to one moment in your life, which would it be and why?

103. Write about the moment you finally realized you were an adult.

104. Write about your secret weakness.

105. Write about a childhood memento you still have to this day.

106. What is your secret source of energy and drive?

107. If your life were a song, what song would it be? Why?

108. Describe your personal brand.

Thank You!

The Mayday writing team sincerely hopes you enjoyed this book and found it to be the antidote to your writer's block woes. If you did enjoy it, we encourage you to leave a review on Amazon to clue others in and to help another writer build productive, creative habits.

Until next time,
The Mayday Writing Collective

Made in the USA
Monee, IL
10 December 2024

73076063R00095